Exercise!

COORDINATION

Catch, Shoot, and Throw Better!

Ellen Labrecque

www.raintreepublishers.co.uk
Visit our website to find out
more information about
Raintree books.

To order:
☎ Phone 0845 6044371
🖷 Fax +44 (0) 1865 312263
🖳 Email myorders@raintreepublishers.co.uk

Customers from outside the UK please telephone +44 1865 312262

Raintree is an imprint of Capstone Global Library
Limited, a company incorporated in England and
Wales having its registered office at 7 Pilgrim Street,
London, EC4V 6LB – Registered company number:
6695582

Text © Capstone Global Library Limited 2013
First published in hardback in 2013
First published in paperback in 2014
The moral rights of the proprietor have been asserted.

Edited by Rebecca Rissman, Daniel Nunn,
and Sian Smith
Designed by Steve Mead
Picture research by Ruth Blair
Production by Victoria Fitzgerald
Originated by Capstone Global Library Ltd
Printed and bound in China by Leo Paper
Products Ltd

ISBN 978 1 406 24203 4 (hardback)
16 15 14 13 12
10 9 8 7 6 5 4 3 2 1

ISBN 978 1 406 24208 9 (paperback)
17 16 15 14 13
10 9 8 7 6 5 4 3 2 1

British Library Cataloguing in Publication Data
Labrecque, Ellen.
   Coordination. -- (Exercise!)
   1. Motor ability--Juvenile literature. 2. Physical
fitness--Juvenile literature. I. Title II. Series
   612.7'6-dc22

Acknowledgements
We would like to thank the following for permission to
reproduce photographs: © Capstone Publishers pp.13,
14, 16, 17, 18, 19, 21, 21, 23 (Karon Dubke); Corbis pp. 7
(© Ocean), 25 (© Ingolf Hatz/cultura), Shutterstock pp.
4 (© Kzenon), 5 (© GeoM), 6 (© Mandy Godbehear),
8 (© Elena Elisseeva), 9 (© goldenangel), 10 (© Juriah
Mosin), 11 (© JJ pixs), 15 (© palko72), 24 (© Galina
Barskaya), 27 (© wavebreakmedia ltd), 27 (© Magone),
28 (© Jules Studio), 29 (© Neale Cousland).

Cover photograph of a tennis player reproduced with
permission of Corbis (© moodboard).

We would like to thank Victoria Gray for her invaluable
help in the preparation of this book.

Contents

Hooray for exercise! 4

What is coordination? 6

Be safe 8

A plus B equals C! 10

The weave 12

Moving backwards 14

Stork stand 16

Walk the line 18

Catching on your back 20

Wall ball 22

Stay cool 24

Eating well 26

Big challenge 28

Glossary 30

Find out more 31

Index 32

Some words are shown in bold, **like this**. You can find out what they mean by looking in the glossary.

Hooray for exercise!

Exercise gives you energy, stretches your muscles, and keeps your bones strong. It can even improve your thinking skills and help you to get a better night's sleep.

It is important to exercise every day.

BY THE NUMBERS
Children should watch
no more than one to
two hours of television
a day.

Exercise also provides you with a strong
immune system to fight off colds and the flu.
Let's get moving!

What is coordination?

There are five different parts of fitness. They are **stamina**, flexibility, strength, speed, and **coordination**. You need coordination for everything you do. Want to catch a ball? Can you skip or score a goal? All these activities use coordination.

You use coordination skills to get a basketball in a hoop.

The good news is that you can become more and more coordinated in any activity or sport. You just have to practise!

...**dinated** doesn't just ...takes time and patience ...en you begin to learn ...fety first. If you want to ...ourself to catch a cricket ball, use a soft ball that won't hurt if it hits you.

Becoming better at sport is brilliant – as long as it is done safely.

BY THE NUMBERS
Between 50 and 80 per cent of all bicycle head injuries could have been prevented if the rider wore a helmet.

Always wear a helmet when you ride a bike or skateboard.

A plus B equals C!

Coordination comes more naturally if you develop your **agility** and **balance** first. Agility is when you are able to move quickly and easily. Balance is when you are able to keep your body upright and steady while you perform skills.

Standing on one leg is a good way to improve your balance.

If you are agile and can stay balanced, activities such as kicking, throwing, and catching become a lot easier!

You need to use agility and balance in sports such as tennis.

The weave

The following game helps with **agility**. Set up six markers in your garden. Place three markers in a straight line about three giant steps apart. In between each set of markers, place another marker about three giant steps to the left.

Sprint from one marker to the next, bending down to touch each one with your hand. You will be moving in a zigzag shape and taking small, quick steps.

MINI CHALLENGE BOX

Try doing "the weave" five times in a row, with small breaks in between each go.

You can use
tall markers or
short markers.
Tall markers are
easier to reach.

Moving backwards

Backpedalling (running backwards) is a great way to develop **agility** and **coordination**. It is tricky to stay **balanced** when your eyes are looking one way and your body is going the other.

On a soft surface such as grass, try backpedalling 50 steps, then **sprint** forwards to get back to where you started.

Make sure you have lots of space behind you before you run backwards.

People need to use backpedalling in many sports, such as tennis and football.

15

Stork stand

Balance is important for developing **coordination**. First, try to develop **static** balance, or balance without moving. Pretend to be a stork. Balance on one leg and see how high you can count to, before you lose your balance.

First, try the stork stand on one leg, and then on the other.

2

MINI CHALLENGE BOX

Whilst balancing on one leg, lift up your other leg, and touch your foot. See if you can hold this for a count of 10. Switch to the other side.

Which leg are you best at balancing on?

17

Walk the line

Find a concrete surface that is smooth and safe to write on with chalk. Draw a straight line with chalk. It should be as long as 10 steps. Walk along the line, placing one foot in front of the other, without "falling off".

Next, try walking backwards along the line to get back to the place where you started.

You can use your arms to help you **balance**.

MINI CHALLENGE BOX

Have fun with the chalk. Draw big dots in a pattern, such as a star or rectangle, and try to jump from one dot to the next. Move your feet as fast as you can!

Catching on your back

Catching a ball is excellent for **hand-eye coordination**. This is when you are able to make your hands react to what your eyes are seeing. A great catching game is to lie on your back with a tennis ball in your hand. Throw the ball in the air with one hand, and try to catch it with the other.

MINI CHALLENGE BOX

See how many times you can throw the ball in the air and catch it without dropping it. Once you reach 15 times, swap hands for the throw and the catch.

21

Wall ball

Stand in front of a concrete wall. Make sure the wall has no windows. Throw a tennis ball against the wall with your right hand, and catch it with your left.

Make sure you throw hard enough to get the ball back into your hand without bouncing.

MINI CHALLENGE BOX

See how many times you can bounce the ball against the wall without dropping it. Once you reach 15 times, swap your throwing and catching hand.

Stay cool

It is important not to overdo things when you exercise. **Heatstroke** is especially dangerous. This is when the body simply cannot get cool. If you start to feel dizzy or sick, have a headache, or feel muscle **cramps**, it is definitely time for a water break!

If you start to feel ill, you need to stop, rest, and drink water.

For the same reasons, always go slower and take it easy during the summer months when the temperature gets hotter.

You need to drink more water when you exercise in hot weather.

Eating well

It is especially important to pick the right things to eat. The healthier you eat, the more energy you'll have to exercise and become more **coordinated**. Can you pick the healthier choice for each meal below?

1. Breakfast
A. Sugared cereal with milk
B. Scrambled eggs and wholemeal toast

2. Lunch
A. Hot dog, chips, fruit juice
B. Wholewheat crackers and cheese, apple slices, yoghurt

3. Dinner
A. Pasta, tomato sauce, carrots, milk
B. Cheeseburger, chips, fizzy drink

There are lots of tasty foods you can eat, that also help your body.

Big Challenge

Tennis is a great sport to play – and it's really fun! It takes **hand-eye coordination** to hit the ball with the racquet, especially when you serve and make overhead shots. You could become a strong player with the right amount of practice, positive thinking, and skill. You'll be hitting the court before you know it! Game, set, match!

Tennis is a fun sport to play outside in the summer.

Professional tennis players practise for about four hours a day.

Glossary

agility ability to stop and change directions very quickly

balance to hold your body steady

coordination ability to get different parts of the body to work well together

cramps pains you can get when muscles tighten suddenly

hand-eye coordination ability to make your hands react to what your eyes are seeing

heatstroke when the body gets too hot and can't cool down

immune system parts of your body that help you fight off illness

protein substance in food that gives the body energy and helps it grow. Eggs, meat, nuts, and beans have protein in them.

sprint run very fast for a short distance

stamina power to keep going or keep doing something

static still or fixed position

Find out more

Books

All About the Olympics, Nick Hunter
(Raintree, 2011)

Exercise (Looking After Me), Claire Llewellyn
(QED, 2008)

Healthy Eating (Health Choices), Cath Senker
(Wayland, 2007)

Websites

news.bbc.co.uk/sport1/hi/academy/default.stm
Find out more about famous people in sport.

www.bam.gov
A website devoted to fitness and health for children,
including exercise, safety, and eating tips.

physicaleducationresources.com/warmups_small_
games_physical_education_resources.aspx
Find out lots of ideas for games and warm ups.

Index

agility 10, 11, 12–13, 14

backpedalling 14–15
balance 10, 11, 14, 16–17, 18
bones 4

coordination 6–7, 10, 14, 16, 20, 28
cramps 24
cycling 9

energy 4

fitness 6
food 26–27

hand-eye coordination 20, 28
head injuries 9
heatstroke 24

helmets 9

immune system 5

muscles 4, 24

safety 8–9, 24–25
skateboarding 9
sprinting 12, 14
static balance 16
stork stand exercise 16–17

television 5
tennis 11, 15, 28–29
throwing and catching a ball 7, 8, 20–21, 22

walking a line 18–19
water 24, 25
weaving 12–13